SYSTEM
administration
Preparing for Network+ Certification

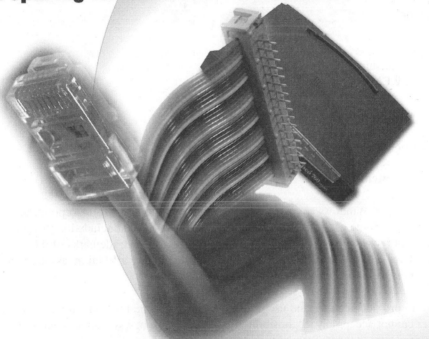

Jerry K. Ainsworth
Shawnee Community College

Kristine A. Kriegel
Technology Trainer and Independent Consultant

EMCParadigm
PUBLISHING

Developmental Editor	Michael Sander, Courtney Kost
Cover Designer	Leslie Anderson
Text Designer	Jennifer Wreisner
Desktop Production	Leslie Anderson, Lisa Beller
Copyeditor	Joy McComb

Publishing Team: George Provol, Publisher; Janice Johnson, Director of Product Development; Tony Galvin, Acquisitions Editor; Lori Landwer, Marketing Manager; Shelley Clubb, Electronic Design and Production Manager.

Text ISBN 0-7638-1975-1
Product Number 03606

© 2004 by Paradigm Publishing Inc.
     Published by **EMC**Paradigm
     875 Montreal Way
     St. Paul, MN 55102

     (800) 535-6865
     E-mail: educate@emcp.com
     Web Site: www.emcp.com

Trademarks: Microsoft and Windows are registered trademarks of the Microsoft Corporation in the United States and other countries. Some of the product names and company names included in this book have been used for identification purposes only and may be trademarks or registered trademarks of their respective manufacturers and sellers. The authors, editor, and publisher disclaim any affiliation, association, or connection with, or sponsorship or endorsement by, such owners.

Care has been taken to provide accurate and useful information about the Internet. However, the author, editor, and publisher cannot accept any responsibility for Web, e-mail, newsgroup, or chat room subject matter or content, or for consequences from any application of the information in this book, and make no warranty, expressed or implied, with respect to the book's content.

Printed in the United States of America
10 9 8 7 6 5 4 3 2 1

WORKBOOK TABLE OF CONTENTS

Contents

Contents   **v**

Contents

PART 1

Media and Topologies

In the first section of the workbook, you will demonstrate your understanding and mastery of the purpose of computer networks, network media, and topologies. By completing the worksheets in this section, you will demonstrate your competence in the following areas:

- Identifying network structures
- Identifying the characteristics of network topologies
- Creating a peer-to-peer network in a star topology with Windows 95 and 98
- Creating a peer-to-peer network in a star topology with Windows 2000 and XP
- Sharing a folder using Windows XP
- Sharing a folder using Windows 95 or 98
- Sharing a printer using Windows 95 or 98
- Functions of the OSI Model layers
- Data movement within the OSI Model
- Matching 802 Committees to their standards
- Matching 802 standards to their characteristics
- Identifying cables and connectors
- Making an unshielded twisted pair straight through cable
- Making an unshielded twisted pair crossover cable
- Making a thin coaxial cable
- Making a thick coaxial cable
- Making a fiber optic cable
- Exploring the inner workings of a hub
- Shopping for network hardware
- Identifying the characteristics of network hardware
- Viewing the configuration of a router

The skills listed above are important to master because they lay the groundwork for the information in the remaining sections. For example, this chapter introduces you to the concept of networks, describes the types of networks commonly used today, and then provides details about the components that are required and how those components should be used. Once you have a solid understanding of the information presented here, not only will you build on to it in the chapters that follow, you will also be able to design and install a network.

1 Logical and Physical Network Topologies

It is important to understand why computers are networked and the common configurations that are used on those networks. Students at all levels should work through these exercises to ensure they understand network topologies and to lay the ground work for later discussions on networking hardware, cables, and components.

Project 1A: Identifying Network Structures

Time to Complete: 20 minutes
Needed: Pen or pencil
Reference: Pages 14-22 of the textbook

1. In the space provided below, draw four personal computers that are networked using a star topology.

2. In the space provided below, draw four personal computers that are networked using a bus topology.

3. In the space provided below, draw four personal computers that are networked using a mesh topology.

4. In the space provided below, draw four personal computers that are networked using a ring topology.

5. In the space provided below, demonstrate your understanding of infrastructure or multipoint wireless networking by drawing a laptop computer and other components required to connect to a fixed network.

6. In the space provided below, demonstrate your understanding of ad hoc wireless networking by drawing two devices communicating.

Project 1B: Identifying the Characteristics of Network Topologies

Time to Complete: 20 minutes
Needed: Pen or pencil
Reference: Pages 14-22 of the textbook

Match each of the following network characteristics with the type of topology.

a. Star   b. Bus   c. Ring   d. Mesh   e. Wireless

_____ 1. Most commonly used for new network installations.

_____ 2. Uses coaxial cable.

_____ 3. Devices connect or network using either ad hoc mode, or infrastructure or multipoint networking.

_____ 4. Each computer is connected directly to every other computer.

_____ 5. Requires termination to eliminate signal bounce.

_____ 6. A "circle" of cable connects each computer to the next.

_____ 7. For every node on the network (n), you will have $n(n-1)/2$ connections.

_____ 8. It is highly fault tolerant.

_____ 9. Token passing is one common method used to transmit data.

_____ 10. The hub can be a single point of failure.

_____ 11. A single break can bring down the entire network.

_____ 12. Considered an active topology.

_____ 13. Nodes connect to a bridge functioning as an access point.

_____ 14. Nodes connect to a multistation access unit (MAU), generally a switch or a hub.

_____ 15. A single length of cable connects each node together in a daisy-chain fashion.

Project 1C: Creating a Peer-to-Peer Network in a Star Topology with Windows 95 and 98

Time to Complete: 30 minutes
Needed: Two or more personal computers running Windows 95 and/or 98, one hub or switch, a twisted pair cable for each computer, and access to the operating system installation files.
Reference: Pages 5 and 14 of the textbook

1. Make the physical connections for the network. As these items are complete, check them off from the list below:
   • Network interface cards properly installed.
   • Cables connected to each network interface card.
   • Cables connected to hub or switch.

2. Check and install the necessary network software:
   • Check the Device Manager to ensure that the NIC is installed and configured correctly.
   • Install the Microsoft Client for Microsoft Networks.
   • Install the NetBEUI protocol.
   • Install File and Print Services for Microsoft Networks.

3. Ensure you have access to operating system installation files, and the driver files for the NIC if they are not on the operating system CD.

4. Check the workgroup configuration:
   • Ensure each of the computers are in the same workgroup.
   • Check and make note of the computer names.

5. After the computers have been restarted, open Network Neighborhood and browse for the other computers in your workgroup. You may need to wait up to ten minutes for all of the computers to appear.

6. Troubleshoot any problems encountered during the process.

Project ID: Creating a Peer-to-Peer Network in a Star Topology with Windows 2000 and XP

Time to Complete: 30 minutes
Needed: Two or more personal computers running Windows 2000 and/or XP, one hub or switch, a twisted pair cable for each computer, and access to the operating system installation files.
Reference: Pages 5 and 14 of the textbook

1. Make the physical connections for the network. As these items are complete, check them off from the list below:
   • Network interface cards properly installed.
   • Cables connected to each network interface card.
   • Cables connected to hub or switch.

2. Check and install the necessary network software:
   • Check the Device Manager to ensure the NIC is installed and configured correctly.
   • Install the Microsoft Client for Microsoft Networks.
   • Install the NetBEUI protocol.
   • Install File and Print Services for Microsoft Networks.

3. Ensure you have access to operating system installation files, and the driver files for the NIC if they are not on the operating system CD.

4. Check the workgroup configuration:
   • Ensure each of the computers are in the same workgroup.
   • Check and make note of the computer names.

5. After the computers have been restarted, open My Network Places and browse for the other computers in your workgroup. You may need to wait up to ten minutes for all of the computers to appear.

6. Troubleshoot any problems encountered during the process.

Project 1E: Sharing a folder with Windows XP

Time to Complete: 30 minutes
Needed: Two or more personal computers running Windows XP that are networked in a peer-to-peer configuration.
Reference: Pages 5-7, 14 of the textbook

1. Open the Windows Explorer utility and create a new folder named My Shared Folder.

2. Copy several files into the folder.

3. Using the mouse, right click on the folder and select Sharing and Security.

4. Share the folder to the network.

5. From another networked computer in your workgroup, browse to the shared folder.

Name: _____

Date: _____

Project 1F: Sharing a folder with Windows 95 or 98

Time to Complete: 30 minutes
Needed: Two or more personal computers running Windows 95 or 98 that are networked in a peer-to-peer configuration.
Reference: Pages 5-7, 14 of the textbook

1. Open the Windows Explorer utility and create a new folder named: My Shared Folder.

2. Copy several files into the folder.

3. Using the mouse, right click on the folder and select Sharing.

4. Share the folder to the network.

5. Notice the permission assignments that are available for the shared resource. Record them here:

6. Select the permission level and assign a password to the shared resource.

7. From another networked computer in your workgroup, browse to the shared folder.

┌─ N O T E ───
│ You may need to wait several minutes for the new share to appear.
└──

Project 1G: Sharing a Printer with Windows 95 or 98

Time to Complete: 30 minutes
Needed: Two or more personal computers running Windows 95 or 98 that are networked in a peer-to-peer configuration. One of the computers needs a printer installed.
Reference: Pages 5-7 of the textbook

1. Open the Printers folder and locate the installed printer.

2. Using the mouse, right click on the printer and select Sharing.

3. Share the printer to the network.

4. Notice the permission assignments that are available for the shared resource. Record them here:

5. Select the permission level and assign a password to the shared resource.

6. From another networked computer in your workgroup, browse to the shared printer.

> **NOTE**
>
> You may need to wait several minutes for the new share to appear.

7. Using the Add Printer Wizard, install the drivers for the shared printer.

8. Print a test page to the printer.

2 The OSI Model

Understanding the OSI Model, and how data communication takes place, can help with troubleshooting communication problems, talking with vendors in the industry, and making decisions concerning which protocols to run and devices to use in your network.

Project 2A: Functions of the Seven Layers of the OSI Model

Time to Complete: 15 minutes
Needed: Pen or pencil
Reference: Page 51 of the textbook

Match the function of the OSI Model layer with the name of the layer.

a. Application layer   d. Transport layer   f. Data Link layer
b. Presentation layer   e. Network layer   g. Physical layer
c. Session layer

_____ 1. Routing

_____ 2. The bus topology

_____ 3. Media Access

_____ 4. Segmentation

_____ 5. Compression/decompression

_____ 6. Point-to-point connections

_____ 7. Character translation

_____ 8. Flow control

_____ 9. Standards for network access

_____ 10. Digital signaling

_____ 11. Reliable transmission

_____ 12. Baseband transmission

_____ 13. CSMA/CD

_____ 14. Encryption/decryption

_____ 15. Physical addressing

_____ 16. Services to computer applications

_____ 17. Logical connections

_____ 18. Bit synchronization

_____ 19. Logical addressing

_____ 20. Conversation setup, maintenance, cessation

Project 2B: Data Movement within the OSI Model

Time to Complete: 5 minutes
Needed: Pen or pencil
Reference: Page 35 of the textbook

1. In the space below, you will find the seven layers of the OSI Model. Using arrows, please draw the three types of communication that can be completed using the framework of the OSI Model.

APPLICATION	APPLICATION
PRESENTATION	PRESENTATION
SESSION	SESSION
TRANSPORT	TRANSPORT
NETWORK	NETWORK
DATA LINK	DATA LINK
PHYSICAL	PHYSICAL

COMPUTER 1   **COMPUTER 2**

3 IEEE Specifications and their Characteristics

Standards typically ensure that products function at the level promised by the manufacturer and also that they will work with other vendor's products. It is necessary to understand the importance of standards and to be able to identify some of the more common networking standards. Students at all levels should work through these exercises to ensure they understand each of the IEEE standards, the technologies to which they relate, and some of their individual characteristics.

Project 3A: Identifying 802 Committees and their Standards

Time to Complete: 20 minutes
Needed: Pen or pencil
Reference: Page 61 of the textbook

Match each of the following committee numbers with the appropriate standard:

a. 802.1	d. 802.4	g. 802.7	j. 802.11	m. 802.16
b. 802.2	e. 802.5	h. 802.9	k. 802.12	n. 802.17
c. 802.3	f. 802.6	i. 802.10	l. 802.15	

_____ 1. Integrated voice/data networks

_____ 2. Metropolitan area networks (MANs)

_____ 3. Network Management

_____ 4. MAC layer standards for Token Ring networks

_____ 5. The Ethernet standard

_____ 6. Broadband wireless standards

_____ 7. General standards for the Logical Link Control sublayer of the Data Link layer

_____ 8. Personal Area networks

_____ 9. MAC layer standards for token passing networks

_____ 10. Network security on local and metropolitan area networks

_____ 11. Broadband local area network standards

_____ 12. Demand Priority Access LAN

_____ 13. Wireless network standards

_____ 14. Resilient packet ring access protocol

Project 3B: Identifying 802 Characteristics

Time to Complete: 20 minutes
Needed: Pen or pencil
Reference: Pages 63-76 of the textbook

Match each of the following committee numbers with the characteristic of their standard:

a. 802.2   b. 802.3   c. 802.5   d. FDDI   e. 802.11

_____ 1. Defines the Carrier Sense Multiple Access with Collision Detection (CSMA/CD) media access method.

_____ 2. A single token travels around the network, from computer to computer.

_____ 3. Defines how network communications should take place within the Logical Link Control (LLC) sublayer.

_____ 4. Can extend to distances up to 60 miles.

_____ 5. Uses a star or bus topology

_____ 6. Acts as an interface between the MAC sublayer and the Network layer of the OSI Model.

_____ 7. One station on the network is selected to be the active monitor.

_____ 8. In ad hoc mode, clients communicate directly with each other.

_____ 9. This type of network is known as deterministic, because the sequence in which stations access the network is predetermined.

_____ 10. A high-speed networking standard originally designed for fiber optic cable.

4 Network Media, Connectors, and their Characteristics

When working with computer networks, either new or existing, you will often be asked to select and install networking components to include cable media. When accomplishing this task, there are many factors to consider. The type of cable you choose will determine the types of connectors and networking hardware that you will need. Students at all levels should work through these exercises to ensure they understand each cable type, their connectors, and their characteristics.

Project 4A: Identify Cables and Connectors

Time to Complete: 20 minutes
Needed: Pen or pencil
Reference: Pages 88-108 of the textbook

Identify each of the following cable and connector types:

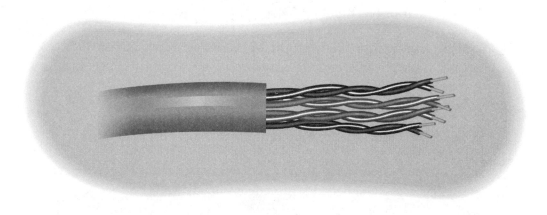

a. _____

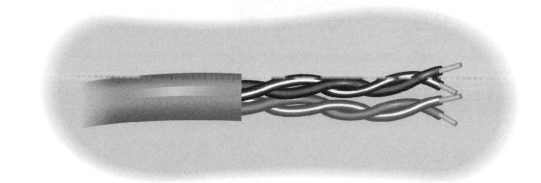

b. _____

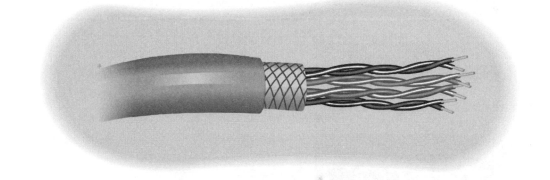

c. _____

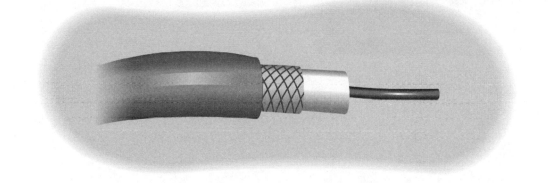

d. _____

e. _____

f. _____

g. _____

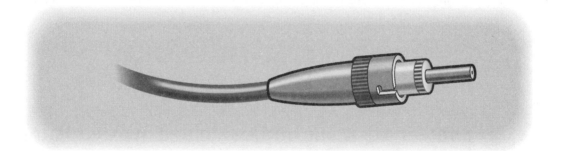

h. _____

i. _____

Project 4B: Make an Unshielded Twisted Pair Straight Through Cable

Twisted Pair Straight Through Cable
Time to Complete: 20 minutes
Needed: Twisted pair cable, RJ-45 connectors, and crimpers
Reference: Pages 91-94 of the textbook

1. Strip the plastic sheath and color-coded protective cover from each of the wires.

2. Consult the pin chart in the chapter.

3. Insert the wires into the RJ-45 connector.

4. Crimp the connector onto the wire.

5. Use a wire tester to confirm that the wire is functioning correctly.

Project 4C: Make an Unshielded Twisted Pair Crossover Cable

Time to Complete: 20 minutes
Needed: Twisted pair cable, RJ-45 connectors, and crimpers
Reference: Page 94 of the textbook

1. Strip the plastic sheath and color-coded protective cover from each of the wires.

2. Consult the pin chart in the chapter.

3. Insert the wires into the RJ-45 connector.

4. Crimp the connector onto the wire.

5. Use a wire tester to confirm that the wire is functioning correctly.

Project 4D: Make a Thick Coaxial Cable

Time to Complete: 20 minutes
Needed: Coaxial cable, AUI connectors, and crimpers
Reference: Pages 103 of the textbook

1. Strip the plastic sheath from the wire.

2. Expose the braided ground.

3. Strip the cover from the center conductor.

4. Fold back the metal braiding.

5. Attach the AUI connector to the wire.

6. Crimp the connector onto the wire.

7. Use a wire tester to confirm that the wire is functioning correctly.

Project 4E: Make a Fiber Optic Cable

Time to Complete: 20 minutes
Needed: Coaxial cable, SC or ST connectors, and crimpers
Reference: Pages 104-106 of the textbook

1. Following the instructions included with the cable or connectors, strip the plastic sheath from the wire.

2. Attach the SC or ST connectors to the wire.

3. Use a media tester to confirm that the cable is functioning correctly.

Name: _____

Date: _____

5 Networking Components

Whether you are involved with large enterprise networks or merely setting up a small network in your home or office, the proper selection of networking components is critical to the success and performance of that network. Students at all levels should work through these exercises to ensure they understand how to select the proper networking components for any given situation.

Project 5A: Explore the Inner Workings of a Hub

Time to Complete: 20 minutes
Needed: Hub and a screwdriver
Reference: Pages 122-123 of the textbook

1. Document the following information about the hub:

   • Manufacturer _____

   • Model _____

   • Serial Number _____

   • Number of ports _____

   • Number and locations of MDIX ports or switches _____

2. Remove the outer cover from a hub.

3. Explore the internal wiring of the hub.

4. Document the port-to-port wiring in the space provided below:

Name: _____

Date: _____

Project 5B: Shopping for Network Hardware

Time to Complete: 30 minutes
Needed: Computer with Internet access
Reference: Pages 122-146 of the textbook

1. Use an Internet search engine such as Google (www.google.com) to locate companies who sell network hardware. Once located, check the specifications and prices of the hardware listed below. In the space provided, record the manufacturer, model number, and price.

   • 12-port 10/100BASE-TX Fast Ethernet hub

   • 24-port Fast Ethernet hub

   • 24-port switch with 100BASEFX ports

   • 8-port token ring hub/multistation access unit

   • Router

   • Bridge

   • Channel Service Unit

   • Data Service Unit

   • Wireless Access Point

Name: _____

Date: _____

Project 5C: Identifying the Characteristics of Network Hardware

Time to Complete: 30 minutes
Needed: Computer with Internet access
Reference: Pages 122-146 of the textbook

Match the network hardware listed below with its characteristic.

_____ 1. Connects multiple network segments together to form a larger network, or large networks together to form an internetwork.

_____ 2. Used to link different network segments, such as Ethernet and Token Ring.

_____ 3. Used to connect dissimilar networks, such as a LAN to a mainframe.

_____ 4. Extends the length of the cable that is being used on the network.

_____ 5. Has the ability to learn the physical addresses of all of the devices on the network.

_____ 6. Works at the Network layer of the OSI Model.

_____ 7. The most basic form of multistation access unit.

_____ 8. The piece of hardware installed inside a computer that allows the computer to be connected to the network.

_____ 9. Widely used before switches were adopted.

_____ 10. Used to establish VLANs.

_____ 11. The unit a wireless network card communicates with in order to connect to the network.

_____ 12. Used to terminate a data line, such as a T1 or T3 line.

Project 5D: Viewing the Configuration of a Router

Time to Complete: 30 minutes
Needed: Computer, serial cable, router
Reference: Pages 133-135 of the textbook

┌─ N O T E ──┐

The exact steps of this exercise will vary depending on the manufacturer of your router. Several
commands are offered in brackets as examples. These will work on most Cisco routers.

└──┘

a. Hubs	d. Routers	g. Network Interface
b. Switches	e. Gateways	Cards
c. Bridges	f. CSU/DSU	h. Wireless access points

1. Connect your computer to the router.

2. Using a terminal program such as HyperTerminal, establish a session with the router.

3. Use the help utility to display many of the available commands. [?]

4. Switch to privileged mode. [enable]

5. Display the running configuration of the router. [show running-config]

6. Display the startup configuration. [show startup-config]

7. Display version information. [show version]

8. Exploring the contents of the router table. [show ip route]

9. Display statistics for all configured interfaces. [show interfaces]

10. Assign a new host name to the router. [hostname]

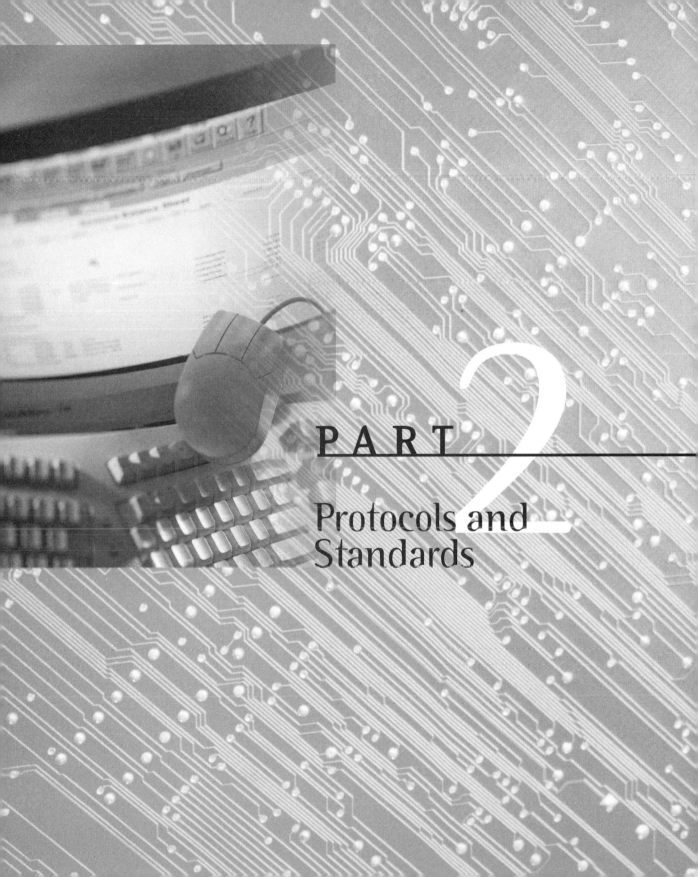

PART 2

Protocols and Standards

In this section of the workbook, you will demonstrate your understanding and mastery of the various protocols that are implemented in networks. You will also identify standards that are common to data networks. By completing the worksheets in this section, you will demonstrate your competence in the following areas:

- Installing the TCP/IP protocol
- TCP/IP logical addressing
- Understanding important IP addresses
- IPX logical addressing
- Installing the NWLink protocol
- Understanding the TCP/IP suite of protocols
- Using FTP
- IMAP and POP3
- Using ARP
- Ports
- IP address classes
- Binary to decimal conversions
- Decimal to binary conversions
- IP address subnetting
- Default subnet masks
- Dynamic addressing
- IP address allocation
- Locating IP address information
- DHCP options
- Installing the DNS service
- Adding host records to the DNS database
- Testing a DNS record
- Configuring the computer for WINS resolution
- Firewall placement
- Determining appropriate WAN technologies
- Circuit switching processes
- Identifying the benefits of ISDN
- Understanding FDDI
- Understanding T-Carriers
- Installing an internal modem
- Creating a new dial-up connection
- Establishing Internet connection sharing
- Installing the routing and remote access service
- Configuring the routing and remote access service
- Using the netsh.exe command-line utility
- Understanding public key infrastructure
- Site-to-site VPNs
- Layer 2 tunneling protocol
- Kerberos process

These skills are important to master because they provide the rules that you must follow in order to build and administer a working network. In addition, this chapter addresses many network software issues which will help you select the correct protocol, client, and service. Finally, the chapter concludes with a chapter that talks about using your knowledge in a remote access situation.

Networking Protocols

As a technician or as a consultant, it is important that you understand the positive and negative features of each of the major protocols used today. You may be asked to assess networks, their operating systems, and connectivity needs, with consideration for which of the protocols will meet the requirements for the networks. By knowing which protocols function with what operating systems, and the characteristics of each protocol, you will be able to make astute judgments about the use of these protocols.

Project 6A: Install the TCP/IP Protocol

Time to Complete: 15 minutes
Needed: One or more personal computers running Windows 2000 Professional and access to the operating system installation files.
Reference: Page 174 of the textbook

1. Open the Network property sheet.

2. Choose the Install button.

3. Choose the protocol you with to install and click the OK button.

4. You will be prompted for the source installation files. Type in the path to the source files and continue.

5. When the TCP/IP protocol property sheet appears, configure the client for dynamic addressing.

Project 6B: TCP/IP Logical Addressing

Time to Complete: 5 minutes
Needed: Pen or pencil
Reference: Pages 178 of the textbook

In the space below, explain the use of logical addressing with protocols designed for networking.

Project 6C: Understanding important addresses

Time to Complete: 5 minutes
Needed: Pen or pencil
Reference: Pages 178 of the textbook

In the following diagram, identify the node IP address and the default gateway for the computers.

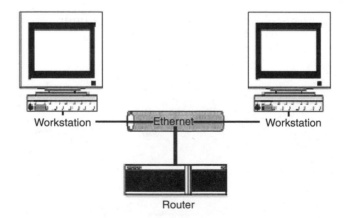

Workstation   Ethernet   Workstation

Router

Project 6D: IPX Logical Addressing

Time to Complete: 1 minute
Needed: Pen or pencil
Reference: Page 186 of the textbook

1. For the following IPX address, identify the network segment address.

    0B0E0D0A:0CCC006798345:456h

    _____

2. Identify which of the following IPX logical addresses is valid by placing a V (valid) or
    N (not valid) next to the address.

    _____ 1. 094GEDB:000000001234

    _____ 2. 08080808:BADDADBEAD12

    _____ 3. 123456789:123456789000

    _____ 4: 08AB86EF00:111111111110

    _____ 5. 0000BED1:11115555BEAD:456h

Project 6E: Install the NWLink Protocol

Time to Complete: 10 minutes
Needed: Personal computer and access to source installation files
Reference: Page 185 of the textbook

1. Open the Network property sheet.
2. Choose the Install button.
3. Choose the protocol you with to install and click the OK button.
4. You will be prompted for the source installation files. Type in the path to the source files
    and continue.

7 TCP/IP

To service clients in the LAN, you must understand the concepts of networking technology including the "languages" computers use to communicate. Understanding the varied TCP/IP protocols and the services and utilities they bring to networking will help you to troubleshoot client problems and take on larger tasks as your experience grows.

Project 7A: Understanding the TCP/IP Suite of Protocols

Time to Complete: 5 minutes
Needed: Pen or pencil
Reference: Pages 209-227 of the textbook

Match each of the following protocols to their function.

a. TFTP	d. POP3/IMAP	g. HTTP	j. ICMP
b. NTP	e. FTP	h. UDP	k. IP
c. TELNET	f. SMTP	i. ARP	l. TCP

_____ 1. Connection-oriented protocol that provide reliable delivery

_____ 2. Connectionless protocol that provides some error checking

_____ 3. Allows sharing of files without regard for operating system

_____ 4. Connectionless transport protocol

_____ 5. Service protocol that guarantees delivery of packets from an email message

_____ 6. File transfer protocol that uses UDP for efficiency

_____ 7. Services for electronic of email messages

_____ 8. Protocol that provides connection to remote host

_____ 9. Stateless, generic protocol for access to Internet resources

_____ 10. Resolves logical address to physical address

_____ 11. Supports time synchronization

_____ 12. Error-response protocol

Project 7B: Using FTP

Time to Complete: 10 minutes
Needed: Personal computer connected to the Internet
Reference: Page 213 of the textbook

Use the FTP protocol to access resources using the anonymous user. Connect to ftp.microsoft.com using "anonymous" as the username and your email address as the password.

Project 7C: IMAP and POP3

Time to Complete: 5 minutes
Needed: Personal computer connected to the Internet, the Outlook email client, and an active email account
Reference: Pages 217-218 of the textbook

1. Check to see if your email is using IMAP or POP3 by opening Outlook, going to the Tools menu, selecting Internet accounts, then Properties.

2. Write in the name of your incoming email server: _____

Project 7D: Using ARP

Time to Complete: 5 minutes
Needed: Personal computer connected to the LAN
Reference: Page 223 of the textbook

1. Open a command prompt and run the ARP utility.

   a. Type **ARP** and read through the switches available.
   b. Choose the switch that will allow you to view the current cache and run that from the command line. Write in the IP addresses of the connections in the space below.
   c. Now use the PING utility to add to the ARP cache.
   d. Run the ARP utility again. Is the IP address you PINGed in Step c in the list?

Project 7E: Ports

Time to Complete: 5 minutes
Needed: Pen or pencil
Reference: Page 227 of the textbook

Protocol	Port Used
TCP	_____
NETSTAT	_____
HTTP	_____
HTTPS	_____
FTP	_____
POP3	_____
SNMP	_____
DNS	_____

IP Addressing

Understanding the format of an IP address will aid you in troubleshooting network connectivity problems. Using pre-configured charts to assign addresses makes some tasks easier, but this does not build the skills that will serve you as you move up the job ladder. By developing an understanding of IP addressing and the options you have in the assignment of those addresses, you can become creative with the addresses available to you and supply all your clients with an address appropriate to the network.

Project 8A: IP Address Classes

Time to Complete: 5 minutes
Needed: Personal computer connected to the Internet
Reference: Page 246 of the textbook

Write an example of an IP address for each of the classes listed below.

Class A _____

Class B _____

Class C _____

Project 8B: Binary to Decimal Conversions

Time to Complete: 10 minutes
Needed: Personal computer connected to the Internet
Reference: Page 241 of the textbook

Convert each of the following binary format IP addresses to decimal.

1. 11010010.11110000.00000001.10101010 _____

2. 00010101.11000011.11111000.11111000 _____

3. 00011101.11100010.11000110.11111111 _____

4. 00000011.00001110.00110011.11000001 _____

5. 01100110.11010011.00001010.11000010 _____

6. 11000110.00111001.10000001.10011100 _____

7. 11100100.11001111.00010111.11000111 _____

8. 01110101.10001010.10101110.01010110 _____

Project 8C: Decimal to Binary Conversions

Time to Complete: 10 minutes
Needed: Personal computer connected to the Internet
Reference: Page 242 of the textbook

Convert each of the following decimal IP addresses to its binary format.

1. 184.251.30.2 _____

2. 123.254.153.147 _____

3. 217.21.45.69 _____

4. 21.51.59.251 _____

5. 238.164.197.22 _____

6. 122.166.177.199 _____

7. 147.195.173.182 _____

8. 222.111.131.144 _____

Project 8D: IP Address Subnetting

Time to Complete: 20 minutes
Needed: Pen or pencil
Reference: Pages 251-257 of the textbook

You are working on a new network that needs an IP addressing scheme. The network has four segments with 22 hosts on the most populated segment. Using the Class C address 201.12.171.0, design a set of subnets to accommodate this network. Include the subnet mask and each of the available network IDs. Use the space below for your work.

Project 8E: More Subnetting

Time to Complete: 15 minutes
Needed: Pen or pencil
Reference: Pages 251-257 of the textbook

Given a Class C address of 220.15.10.0, and a subnet mask of 255.255.255.240, build the first four subnet network addresses. Use the space below for your work.

Project 8F: Default Subnet Masks

Time to Complete: 5 minutes
Needed: Pen or pencil
Reference: Page 250 of the textbook

Identify the default subnet mask for each of the following IP addresses:

1. _____ 10.20.30.122

2. _____ 174.24.62.3

3. _____ 121.251.41.39

4. _____ 45.65.49.253

5. _____ 215.243.156.78

6. _____ 87.92.199.62

7. _____ 199.189.179.159

8. _____ 167.59.89.77

9. _____ 223.3.33.133

10. _____ 158.167.45.1

9 Network Services

Every network makes use of additional services that are provided either by devices or the network operating system software itself. These services allow computers to find each other on the network, receive IP addresses, or monitor events that occur within devices attached to the network. It is important for the technician to understand each service and how it functions on the network.

Project 9A: Dynamic Addressing

Time to Complete: 5 minutes
Needed: Pen or Pencil
Reference: Page 277 of the textbook

In the following diagram, label each step to acquire an IP address dynamically.

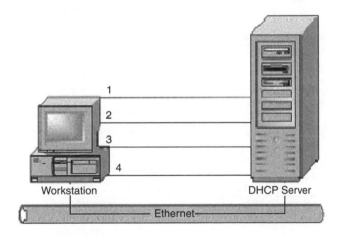

Project 9B: IP Address Allocation

Time to Complete: 5 minutes
Needed: Pen or Pencil
Reference: Page 276 of the textbook

In the following diagram, use the list of addresses to identify which address each computer might expect to acquire if all workstations are set to use DHCP. The IP address of the server is 201.165.22.79.

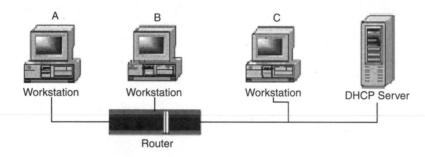

1. 184.251.30.2   _____

2. 201.165.114.56   _____

3. 201.165.22.46   _____

4. 201.165.115.56   _____

5. 169.254.0.10   _____

6. 169.254.0.11   _____

7. 169.254.0.12   _____

Project 9C: DHCP Options

Time to Complete: 5 minutes
Needed: Pen or pencil
Reference: Page 276 of the textbook

You have two servers and three printers on a segment where TCP/IP is used for communication. Your segment uses DHCP. The servers and printers must always use the same IP address. How will you accomplish this without manually configuring an address on each machine?

Name: _____

Date: _____

Project 9D: Install the DNS Service on a Windows 2000 Server

Time to Complete: 15 minutes

Needed: Personal computer, access to the Windows 2000 Server operating system files

Reference: Page 283 of the textbook

Add the DNS service to a Windows 2000 server:

1. Open Control Panel and locate Add/Remove Programs.

2. Click on the Add/Remove Windows Components.

3. In the *Windows Components* window, scroll to Networking Services.

4. Click the Details button.

5. Check the Domain Name System (DNS) box and click OK.

6. Click Next and wait for the service to install.

7. Open the DNS management console.

8. Right-click on the Forward Lookup Zone and choose New Zone.

9. For Zone Type, choose Primary.

10. For Name, enter the following: [*your name*].com and click Next.

11. Click Next on the *Zone File* window.

12. Click Finish to complete the zone creation.

N O T E

In order to have a functioning DNS server, you will also have to create the reverse lookup zone. The wizard will guide you through this process.

Project 9E: Add a Host Record to the DNS Database

Time to Complete: 15 minutes

Needed: Personal computer running Windows 2000 Server, DNS service installed

Reference: Page 284 of the textbook

Add a Host (A) record to the DNS database:

1. Open the DNS management console.

2. Expand the tree until you see the forward lookup zone for your zone.

3. Right-click on your zone and choose New Host.

4. Type in the name of another computer using the domain name created in Project 9A. (i.e. *[computername]*.*[yourdomain]*.com.

5. Add the IP address of the computer and click Add Host.

6. Choose Done when the record is added.

7. Locate the record in the details pane of the management console.

Project 9F: Test the DNS Record

Time to Complete: 5 minutes
Needed: Personal computer running the Windows 2000 operating system (Server or Professional)
Reference: Page 288 of the textbook

Test the DNS record you added in Project 9B:

1. Open a command prompt window.
2. PING the computer you added in the last project by IP address.
3. Next, ping the computer using its host name.
4. Record your results below.

Project 9G: Configure the Computer for WINS Resolution

Time to Complete: 20 minutes
Needed: Personal computer running the Windows 2000 operating system (Server or Professional)
Reference: Page 288 of the textbook

Configure a Windows 2000 machine to use WINS for NetBIOS to IP address resolution:

1. From Control Panel, choose Add/Remove Programs, Add/Remove Windows Components.
2. Under *Networking Services,* choose Windows Internet Name Service (WINS) by checking the box.
3. Complete the installation.
4. Open the WINS management console.
5. Record below the status of the WINS service.

10 Public vs. Private Networks

Project 10A: Firewall Placement

Time to Complete: 10 minutes
Needed: Pen or pencil
Reference: Page 307 of the textbook

In the space provided below, draw one diagram that includes the following:

a. Two computers within the private network
b. A web server resource within the public network
c. The location of the firewall

11 WAN Technologies

In today's business market, virtually every business you encounter makes use of some kind of wide area network technology. It may be as simple as connecting one office to the Internet, or as complex as connecting many international sites. As a technician, it is important that you understand the technologies used to provide these interconnections and what considerations can influence decisions to use one or the other for a particular situation.

Project 11A: Determining Appropriate WAN Technologies

Time to Complete: 15 minutes
Needed: Pen or pencil
Reference: Pages 332-347 of the textbook

You have been asked by your supervisor to make a recommendation for connecting several sites of a business. Given the facts below, determine which type or types of WAN connectivity will best suit the situation. Justify your reasoning. Use the space below the facts for your answer and justification.

Facts:
- Seven locations, all within the United States
- Corporate headquarters located in Oleatha, Kansas
- Remote locations in Bismarck, North Dakota; Albany, New York; Green Bay, Wisconsin; Huntersville, North Carolina; Destin, Florida; Sedona, Arizona
- Manufacturing business with plants at all locations except Oleatha, Kansas
- Network uses Windows 2000 servers and workstations
- Plant data must be sent to corporate headquarters every 12 hours
- All locations have Internet access
- All locations use Exchange 2000 for e-mail and can receive and send e-mail to and from external sources
- A second failover system must also be in place

Project IIB: Circuit Switching Processes

Time to Complete: 15 minutes
Needed: Pen or pencil
Reference: Page 333 of the textbook

List in the space below the six (6) steps to negotiate transmission in a circuit switched network.

1.

2.

3.

4.

5.

6.

Project 11C: Identifying the Benefits of ISDN

Time to Complete: 10 minutes
Needed: Pen or pencil
Reference: Page 337 of the textbook

Below, list four (4) benefits of ISDN service.

Project 11D: Understanding FDDI

Time to Complete: 15 minutes
Needed: Pen or pencil
Reference: Page 337 of the textbook

Draw an FDDI network with four stations attached to the network. Mark them A, B, C, and D. Use the space provided for your drawing. Use a different colored pen or pencil to indicate what happens to the network when station B fails.

Project 11E: Understanding T-Carriers

Time to Complete: 5 minutes
Needed: Pen or pencil
Reference: Page 346 of the textbook

Next to each T-Carrier type listed below, list the speed of transmission for that carrier type.

T1   _____

T3   _____

E1   _____

E3   _____

OC3   _____

OC12   _____

12 Remote Access Protocols, Services, and Troubleshooting

As a network technician, you will be called on to install and maintain remote access hardware and software on both clients and servers. In addition, you can expect many support calls from remote access users when they are unable to connect or access network resources. Students at all levels should work through these exercises to ensure they understand how to select the proper networking components for any given situation.

Project 12A: Install an Internal Modem

Time to Complete: 20 minutes
Needed: Personal computer, modem, screwdriver, and an ESD wrist strap
Reference: Page 145 of the textbook

1. Remove the cover from the computer and attach the ESD wrist strap.

2. Insert the modem into the computer.

3. Install the cover on the computer.

4. Reconnect any components, plug in the power, and turn the computer on.

5. If the operating system finds the new hardware, supply the path to the installation (driver) files.

6. If the operating system does not find the newly installed modem, re-check the installation.

7. If necessary, use the Add Hardware Wizard located in the Control Panel.

8. Attach a cable from a wall jack to the modem.

9. Open the Device Manager and review the resource settings for the modem. Record the settings in the spaces provided below:

   • IRQ   _____

   • Memory Range _____

   • I/O Range   _____

   • COM Port   _____

   • Maximum port speed   _____

Project 12B: Create a New Dial-Up Connection

Time to Complete: 20 minutes
Needed: Personal computer, installed modem, attached phone line, ISP
Reference: Pages 375-378 of the textbook

1. Use the Network Connections Wizard to create a new dial-up connection.

2. Select the Dial-up to the Internet option.

3. Set up the Internet connection manually.

4. Enter the area code and telephone number of your ISP.

5. Select the correct protocol to support your connection: PPP, Serial Line Internet Protocol (SLIP), or Compressed Serial Line Internet Protocol (CSLIP).

6. Choose your logon procedure and assignment of IP and DNS addresses.

7. Enter a username and password to log on to the ISP server.

8. Click on the Dial button to establish your connection.

9. Test your connection to the ISP.

Project 12C: Install the Routing and Remote Access Service

Time to Complete: 40 minutes
Needed: A server or computer running the Microsoft Windows 2000 Server network operating system.
Reference: Pages 363-368 of the textbook

1. In Administrative Tools, locate Routing and Remote Access.

2. On the Action menu, select Configure and Enable Routing and Remote Access.

3. Follow the steps provided by the Routing and Remote Access Server Setup Wizard.

4. At the Common Configurations screen, select Remote Access Server.

5. When the Remote Access Server Setup screen appears, select Basic remote access server.

6. Verify that all of the protocols you want to support at the dial-up connection are listed. Ensure that TCP/IP is installed.

7. Create a range of IP addresses for the server to distribute.

Project 12D: Configure the Routing and Remote Access Service

Time to Complete: 40 minutes
Needed: A server or computer running the Microsoft Windows 2000 Server network operating system.
Reference: Pages 368-375 of the textbook

1. Once the RRAS service is installed on your server, view and record the settings for each of the five available property sheets.

   • General _____

   • Security _____

   • IP   _____

   • PPP   _____

   • Event Logging _____

2. Enable Event logging.

Project 12E: Use the Netsh.exe Command-line Utility

Time to Complete: 40 minutes
Needed: A server or computer running a Microsoft Windows operating system.
Reference: Page 375 of the textbook

1. To view help, type **Netsh /?** at the command prompt.
2. Explore the available options.
3. Display a configuration script.
4. Change to the RAS context.
5. To display additional information, type **netsh show**.

13 Security Protocols

As a technician, it is important that you understand the various security options available to networks and be able to assess the need to use one form or another in given situations.

Project 13A: Public Key Infrastructure

Time to Complete: 10 minutes
Needed: Pen or pencil
Reference: Page 339 of the textbook

In the space provided below, explain the process used by Public Key Infrastructure to protect data. Be sure to include all key components.

Project 13B: Virtual Private Networks

Time to Complete: 10 minutes
Needed: Pen or pencil
Reference: Page 402 of the textbook

Draw a site-to-site VPN connection, including all elements, in the space below.

Project 13C: Layer 2 Tunneling Protocol

Time to Complete: 10 minutes
Needed: Pen or pencil
Reference: Page 404 of the textbook

In the space below, list the five-step process for L2TP encapsulation.

Project 13D: Kerberos

Time to Complete: 15 minutes
Needed: Pen or pencil
Reference: Page 410 of the textbook

Explain the Kerberos ticketing process, making sure to include all elements. If a drawing is more helpful, use the space provided to include a pictorial explanation.

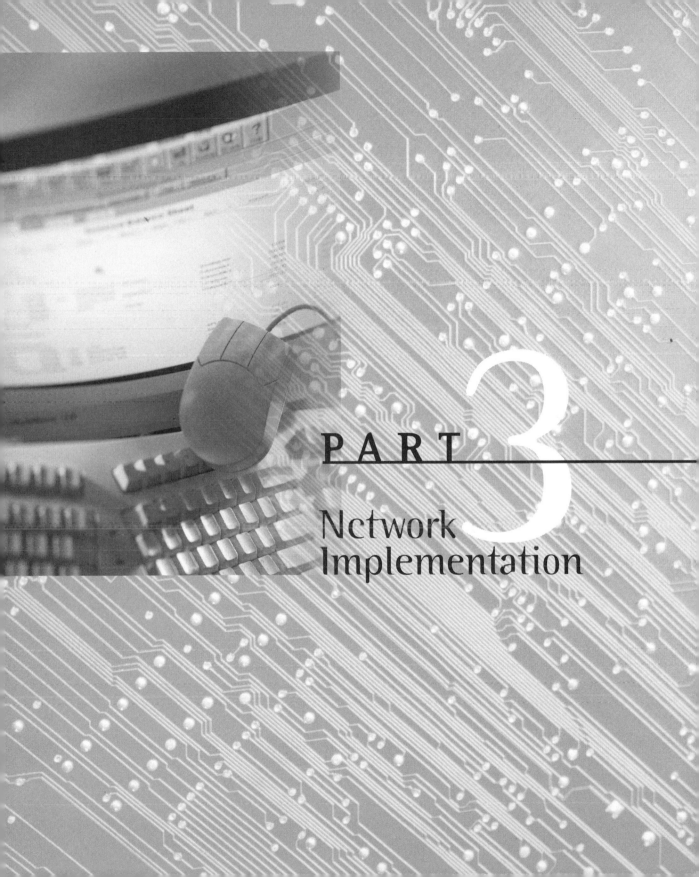

PART 3

Network Implementation

In this section of the workbook, you will demonstrate your understanding and mastery of how to implement a network. You will learn the high points of several network operating systems, how to ensure network integrity, and how to configure a client to communicate on a network. By completing the worksheets in this section, you will demonstrate your competence in the following areas:

- Choosing a network operating system
- Installing the Windows 2000 Server operating system
- Network documentation
- Disaster recovery
- Testing a UPS
- Installing a network interface card
- Installing the Microsoft Client for Microsoft networks
- Configuring the client for Microsoft networks to log on to a domain
- Configuring the client for Microsoft networks to log on to a workgroup
- Installing and configuring the Novell client for NetWare networks
- Installing and configuring the TCP/IP Protocol
- Editing and testing the LMHosts file
- Editing the hosts file

These skills are important to master because they stress the benefits of the most popular network operating systems and when they should be implemented. In addition, information is provided to help recover your network in the event of a catastrophe. The chapter concludes with a discussion and instructions for connecting a client workstation to a network.

14 Network Operating Systems

In order for the network technician to fully understand data communications, it is important that he or she understand the operating systems that allow users to access resources or that restrict user access. Along with that understanding comes an appreciation for the choice of network operating system and the reasons for choosing one over another.

Project 14A: Choosing a Network Operating System

Time to Complete: 10 minutes
Needed: Pen or pencil
Reference: Pages 435-465 of the textbook

For each of the brief scenarios listed, determine which network operating system would be most appropriate and justify your answer. Some scenarios may be appropriate for more than one NOS. Not all operating systems will be used.

Your choices are: Windows 9x (NetBEUI)
                           UNIX
                           NetWare 5.x
                           Windows NT
                           Windows 2000
                           Macintosh

Scenario 1:   Company ABC is a small startup with 6 users. The office is not connected to the Internet. Users share 2 printers. This company does some work for the government, and must maintain the integrity of certain files. Company ABC cannot afford any equipment other than the employees' PCs. Any operating system chosen must be able to run standard software used by employees.

Scenario 2: The Border Company is a well-established enterprise network with approximately 3,000 users. There are offices located in three geographically distant cities. Security is a major concern for the Border Company. Some data is highly sensitive and must be protected from all but a few users. The equipment that will be used as servers (they need at least eight due to software and large data storage needs) will be maintained in a climate-controlled locked room. TCP/IP is used for communication across the enterprise.

Scenario 3: The Artful Company is a graphic arts studio that produces artwork for print media. Most users are comfortable with the software they use for production, but none is truly technical. The network operating system must be easy to manage. Although files are shared as well as printers, the files should be maintained on a central server.

Project 14B: Installing Windows 2000 Server
(may be done as a demonstration)

Time to Complete: 50 minutes
Needed: Computer that meets Windows 2000 minimum requirements (see below), Windows 2000 server operating system source installation files.
Reference: Page 456 of the textbook

This project assists you in the installation of Windows 2000 Server. Only basic information is given. Be sure to watch the process of installation and note when the text portion of the installation ends and the GUI portion begins.

Minimum Requirements: Processor – 133 MHz Pentium
Memory – 64 MB (128 MB recommended)
Disk Space – 1 GB (2 GB recommended)
Monitor – VGA or higher
Additional equipment – CD-ROM drive, Mouse or pointing device

Server Name: SERVER1
Disk Partition: (at least) 1 GB
File System: NTFS

N O T E

Be sure to record the product key before beginning the installation.

N O T E

The computer where Windows 2000 will be installed should be removed from the network to avoid any conflicts with the production network.

Name: _____

Date: _____

1. To begin the installation, place the Windows 2000 Server CD in the CD-ROM drive and reboot the computer (if this does not work, edit the BIOS to boot from the CD-ROM). The installation will begin when the computer boots from the CD-ROM.

2. Allow the file copy to progress

3. Once the file copy has completed, the computer will restart and begin the GUI-mode portion of the installation. During this phase, information about the computer will be recorded by the operating system.

4. Configure the Regional Settings to reflect your locale.

5. If the product key screen appears, enter the key now.

6. Configure the server for five "Per Server" licenses

7. Enter the server name when prompted.

8. Leave the Administrator Password blank. (This is done only for this exercise. In a production environment, be sure to enter a complex password here).

9. When the Network Settings screen appears, configure the system for TCP/IP. Configure the IP address manually as 192.168.10.1. Use the default subnet mask.

10. Make the server part of the workgroup "WORKGROUP1."

11. When the Installation Wizard has completed the installation, click the Finish button.

15 Network Integrity

As a network technician, you will be asked to do many of the everyday tasks that keep the network running. Most of those tasks have a direct effect on the integrity of the network. It is important that you understand the methods and options as well as the necessary tasks that keep the network running smoothly. Pay close attention to power management and backup operations as you will see these areas in the field often.

Project 15A: Network Documentation (Team Lab)

Time to Complete: 30 minutes
Needed: Pen or pencil, paper
Reference: Page 482 of the textbook

Choose from one to three other students to create a documentation team. Using the criteria you have learned, create a network document. Include the following components in the report:

- LAN/WAN topology
- Hardware
- Software
- Server information
- Router and switch configuration
- User policies and profiles (if appropriate)
- Baseline documentation
- Network service configuration
- Change log

Project 15B: Disaster Recovery
(Can be done as a team lab)

Time to Complete: 30-60 minutes
Needed: Pen or pencil, paper
Reference: Page 484 of the textbook

If instructed to do so, pick a student partner to complete this lab.

Design a disaster recovery plan for the classroom network. Include the following:
- Risks, threats, and vulnerabilities
- Business Impact Assessment (BIA)
- Definition of needs
- Detailed plan of action when a disaster is encountered

Project 15C: Test a UPS (Can be done as a demonstration)

Time to Complete: 15 minutes
Needed: Functioning Uninterruptible Power Supply connected to a workstation
Reference: Page 488 of the textbook

1. Confirm that the UPS is connected to a workstation and properly configured.
2. Remove the UPS power cord from the electrical outlet while the workstation is running.
3. Record what occurs when you complete Step 2.
4. If your instructor permits, allow the workstation to run on the power provided by the UPS. Record what happens below.

16 Client Workstation Basics

One of the primary jobs that a Network+ certified technician will perform is connecting client computers to a network. The first step is to install the hardware and software necessary to connect to the network. Once these components are installed, there are many configuration steps that are required, and these steps vary from network to network, client to client. Students at all levels should work through these exercises to ensure they understand how to install and configure client hardware and software.

Project 16A: Install a Network Interface Card

Time to Complete: 20 minutes
Needed: Personal computer, network interface card, screwdriver, and an ESD wrist strap
Reference: Pages 518-521 of the textbook

1. Remove the cover from the computer and attach the ESD wrist strap.

2. Insert the network card into the computer.

3. Install the cover on the computer.

4. Reconnect any components, plug in the power, and turn the computer on.

5. If the operating system finds the new hardware, supply the path to the installation (driver) files.

6. If the operating system does not find the newly installed network card, re-check the installation.

7. If necessary, use the Add Hardware Wizard located in the Control Panel.

8. Attach a cable from a wall jack to the card.

9. Open the Device Manager and review the resource settings for the network card. Record the settings in the spaces provided below:

- IRQ _____

- Memory Range _____

- I/O Range _____

- COM Port _____

- Maximum port speed _____

Project 16B: Install the Microsoft Client for Microsoft Networks

Time to Complete: 10 minutes
Needed: Personal computer, access to the operating system installation files
Reference: Pages 524-525 of the textbook

1. Open the Network property sheet.

2. Select the client you wish to install and press the OK button.

3. You will be prompted for the source installation files. Type in the path to the source files.

Project 16C: Configure the Client for Microsoft Networks to Log on to a Domain

Time to Complete: 10 minutes

Needed: Personal computer, access to the operating system installation files

Reference: Pages 525-529 of the textbook

1. Open the Control Panel and locate the System icon.

2. When the System Properties sheet appears, select the Computer Name tab.

3. At the Computer Name property sheet, locate and click the Network ID button.

4. The Network Identification Wizard appears.

5. At the Connecting to the Network dialog box, select *My company uses a network with a domain.*

6. Provide the information that is required to add a computer to the domain. Ensure you have this information before proceeding.

7. When the process has completed, restart the computer for the change to be effective.

Project 16D: Configure the Client for Microsoft Networks to Log on to a Workgroup

Time to Complete: 10 minutes

Needed: Personal computer, access to the operating system installation files

Reference: Pages 529-530 of the textbook

1. Open the Control Panel and locate the System icon.

2. Select the Computer Name tab.

3. Use the Network Identification Wizard to select the option stating *This computer is part of a business network and I use it to connect to the other computers at work.*

4. At the Connecting to the Network dialog box, select *My company uses a network without a domain.*

5. Provide the name of your workgroup.

6. Restart the computer.

Project 16E: Install and Configure the Novell Client for NetWare Networks

Time to Complete: 20 minutes
Needed: Personal computer with Internet Access, access to the operating system installation files, Novell client installation files
Reference: Pages 531-532 of the textbook

1. Download the self-extracting executable file.

2. Extract the files and locate the Setupnw.exe file which will be located in the Temp directory.

3. At the Installation Option screen, select Typical Installation.

4. When prompted, restart the computer.

5. Once the computer restarts, you will be prompted for the following information:

   • Username _____

   • Password _____

   • Novell Directory Services tree _____

   • Novell Directory Services context _____

   • Server name _____

6. This information can be obtained from your network administrator.

Project 16F: Install and Configure the TCP/IP Protocol

Time to Complete: 20 minutes
Needed: Personal computer with Internet Access, access to the operating system installation files
Reference: Pages 538-543 of the textbook

1. Using the Network property, install the Internet Protocol (TCP/IP).
2. Record the following information in the space provided below:

   • IP Address _____

   • Subnet Mask _____

   • Default Gateway _____

   • DNS Server _____

   • WINS Server _____

3. Open the TCP/IP properties page.
4. Enter all the information recorded above into the appropriate place on the properties page.
5. When you have finished adding information, click the OK button and exit out of Network properties.
6. Restart the computer.
7. Test your configuration using the ping command.

   • PING a host on your subnet by IP address.

   • PING a host on your local subnet by name.

   • PING a host located on the Internet using the host's IP address.

   • PING a host located on the Internet using the fully qualified domain name.

Project 16G: Edit and Test the LMHosts File

Time to Complete: 20 minutes

Needed: Personal computer with a Microsoft Windows operating system. The computer should be configured in a workgroup with at least two other computers.

Reference: Pages 553-554 of the textbook

1. Attempt to connect, by name, with one of the other computers in your workgroup. The attempt should be unsuccessful.
2. Record the name and IP addresses of two computers in the space provided below:

   • Computer 1: _____   _____

   • Computer 2: _____   _____

3. Locate and open the sample LMHosts file.
4. Add entries for the two computers identified above.
5. Make the appropriate entries so that one computer can be preloaded into cache.
6. Specify the name of your domain.
7. Save the file as "LMHosts" without an extension.
8. Restart the computer.
9. Attempt to connect, by name, with one of the other computers in your workgroup. You should now be able to connect.

Project 16H: Edit the Hosts File

Time to Complete: 20 minutes

Needed: Personal computer with a Microsoft Windows operating system.

Reference: Pages 548-549 of the textbook

1. Record the name and IP addresses of two computers in the space provided below:

   • Computer 1: _____   _____

   • Computer 2: _____   _____

2. Locate and open the Hosts file.
3. Add entries for two other computers
4. Edit the entries to include several different case variations of the name.
5. Save the Hosts file.
6. Restart the computer.

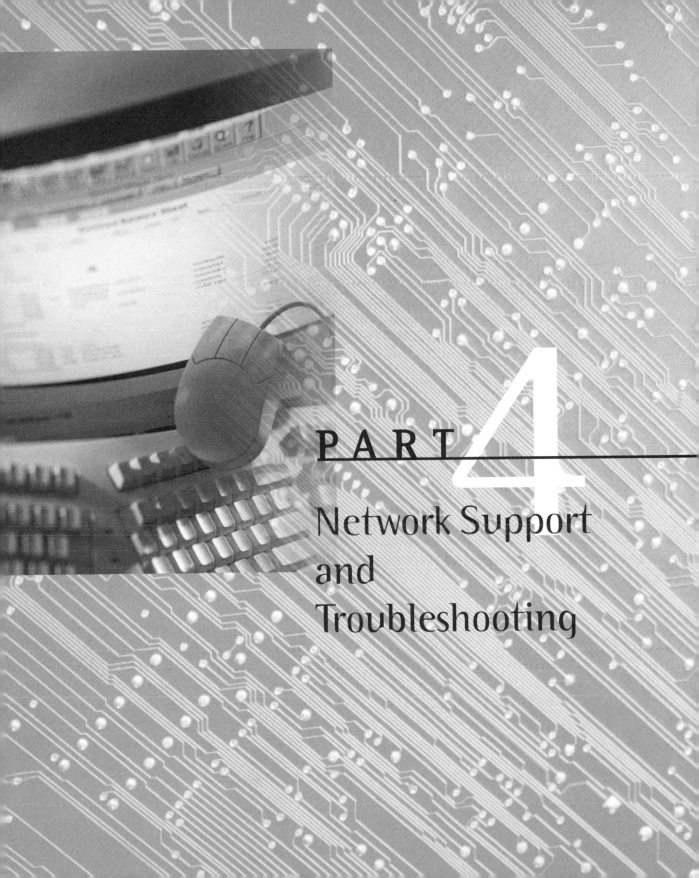

PART 4

Network Support and Troubleshooting

In this section of the workbook, you will demonstrate your understanding and mastery of supporting an existing network and troubleshooting problems as they occur. The section begins by discussing how to approach problems in a structured manner, and then progresses through the use of various tools and utilities. By completing the worksheets in this section, you will demonstrate your competence in the following areas:

- Identifing the affected area
- Establishing what has changed
- Selecting the most probable cause
- Testing the result
- Documenting your solution
- Shopping for network troubleshooting tools
- Using wire crimpers to attach BNC connectors to thin coaxial cable
- Using a media tester to test twisted pair cable
- Using a punch down tool
- Using tracert for troubleshooting
- Using PING for troubleshooting
- Using address resolution protocol
- Using Netstat
- Using Nbtstat
- Using IPCONFIG
- Using WINIPCFG
- Shopping for DSL service
- Connecting a personal computer to DSL service
- Shopping for cable service
- Connecting a personal computer to a cable service
- Shopping for satellite service
- Connecting a personal computer to a wireless network
- Creating an ad hoc wireless network
- Troubleshooting a modem with AT commands

These skills are important to master because they provide focus for tackling network problems in a structured, common sense manner. The chapter also identifies and discusses various tools that can help with your troubleshooting efforts. It outlines various utilities that are available to use in certain trouble-shooting situations. It concludes with a discussion that is focused on troubleshooting problems that are particular to small office and home office environments.

17 Using a Structured Troubleshooting Strategy

Troubleshooting is more than just fixing problems. It is the process of taking a large, complex problem, and through the use of various techniques, excluding all potential elements until only the actual cause remains. Once the actual cause is identified, it can then be fixed. Students at all levels should work through these exercises to ensure they understand how to work through and solve typically network related problems.

Project 17A: Establishing the Symptoms of a Problem

Time to Complete: 30 minutes
Needed: Pen
Reference: Pages 587 of the textbook

1. A user has called the help desk to report that his computer will not work. Develop questions designed to establish the symptoms of the problem.

2. List five open-ended questions.

   •

   •

   •

-

-

3. List five closed-ended questions.

-

-

-

-

-

Project 17B: Identify the Affected Area

Time to Complete: 20 minutes
Needed: Pen
Reference: Page 589 of the textbook

1. Two users have called the help desk to report that they cannot log onto the network. Develop questions designed to identify the affected area of the problem.

2. List three questions you might logically ask to identify the scope of the problem.

   •

   •

   •

Project 17C: Establish what has Changed

Time to Complete: 20 minutes
Needed: Pen
Reference: Pages 589-591 of the textbook

1. A user has called the help desk to report that she can no longer view web pages on the Internet. She also reports that three days ago, a new service pack was installed on her computer. Develop questions designed to identify the affected area of the problem.

2. List three questions you might logically ask to troubleshoot this problem.

   •

   •

   •

3. List three questions you might logically ask in order to recreate the problem.

   •

   •

   •

Project 17D: Select the Most Probable Cause

Time to Complete: 20 minutes
Needed: Pen
Reference: Pages 591-597 of the textbook

1. Based on the information developed in 17C, what is the most probable cause?

2. List three items you can eliminate.

    •

    •

    •

3. List three tools you may use to troubleshoot this problem.

    •

    •

    •

Project 17E: Test the Result

Time to Complete: 20 minutes
Needed: Pen
Reference: Pages 599-600 of the textbook

1. Based on the information developed in 17D, test the result of your proposed solution.

2. List three tests you might perform to test your proposed solution.

   •

   •

   •

3. List three potential side effects of your proposed solution.

   •

   •

   •

Name: _____

Date: _____

Project 17F: Document your Solution

Time to Complete: 30 minutes
Needed: Pen
Reference: Pages 601-602 of the textbook

1. Document the solution for projects 17C - 17E for inclusion in a knowledgebase.

   • Technician's name: _____

   • Date and time: _____

   • Caller's name and phone number: _____

   • Type of computer hardware: _____

   • Operating system: _____

   • Service packs applied: _____

   • If software-related, name and version of software: _____

   • Nature of the problem: _____

   • Troubleshooting steps used: _____

   • Solution: _____

   • Date and time that problem was resolved: _____

   • Total time involved: _____

18 Network Troubleshooting Tools

Technicians in all fields need a good set of tools. This is equally true when working in a network environment where problems are bound to occur. Additionally, the technicians must understand how to properly use each of those tools. Students at all levels should work through these exercises to ensure they understand which tool to select in a given situation and how to properly use it.

Project 18A: Shopping for Network Troubleshooting Tools

Time to Complete: 30 minutes
Needed: A PC with Internet access
Reference: Pages 616-625 of the textbook

1. Search the Internet to locate the following items. Record the vendor, price, and model name or number of each in the space provided:

• Technician's tool kit:

_____

• Field technician's tool kit:

_____

• Wire crimpers:

_____

• Media tester:

_____

. • Time Domain Reflectometer:

_____

• Optical tester:

_____

• Punch down tool:

_____

• Tone generator:

_____

Project 18B: Use Wire Crimpers to Attach BNC Connectors to Thin Coaxial Cable

Time to Complete: 30 minutes
Needed: A length of thin coaxial cable, two BNC connectors, and a pair of wire crimpers
Reference: Pages 617-619 of the textbook

1. Use the crimpers to make two clean cut, straight ends on the cable.
2. Strip the outer cover from the cable.
3. Peel back the outer conductive metal braiding.
4. Attach a BNC connector to both ends of the cable.
5. Select the appropriate cavity on the crimpers and crimp the connectors on to the wire.
6. Test the newly created wire.

Project 18C: Use a Media Tester to Test Twisted Pair Cable

Time to Complete: 30 minutes

Needed: A straight through twisted pair cable and a crossover twisted pair cable

Reference: Pages 619-621 of the textbook

1. Follow the instructions for the media tester.
2. Attach the straight through cable.
3. Use the media tester to check the straight through cable.
4. Attempt to check as many of the following items as available with your cable tester:
   - Continuity
   - Crosstalk
   - Noise
   - Attenuation
   - Capacitance
5. Attach the crossover cable.
6. Use the media tester to check the crossover cable.

Project 18D: Use a Punch Down Tool

Time to Complete: 30 minutes

Needed: Punch down tool, a length of twisted pair cable, and a punch down block or patch panel

Reference: Page 623 of the textbook

1. Strip the outer covering from the twisted pair cable.
2. Place individual wires across clips on the punch down block or patch panel.
3. Attach the wires to the clips.
4. Trim the excess wire if necessary.

19 Troubleshooting Network Problems Using TCP/IP

The TCP/IP protocol is probably one of the least user-friendly protocols in operation on modern networks. It is also the most commonly used protocol. Therefore, it is not only important to understand how to install and configure it, but it is equally important to understand the tools available to troubleshoot problems that are bound to occur. Fortunately, the TCP/IP protocol suite contains many tools—both command line and graphical—to help you troubleshoot problems as they arise. Students at all levels should work through these exercises to ensure they understand which utility to select in a given situation and how to properly use it.

Project 19A: Use Tracert for Troubleshooting

Time to Complete: 20 minutes
Needed: A PC with Internet access
Reference: Pages 638-639 of the textbook

1. Trace your traffic using an IP address of an Internet host. Record the results in the space below:

2. Trace your packet traffic to a fully qualified domain name. Record the results in the space below:

3. Use the appropriate switch to instruct Tracert to not resolve IP addresses to hostnames. What is the benefit of using this switch?

4. Specify the maximum number of hops to use while searching for the target host.

Project 19B: Use PING for Troubleshooting

Time to Complete: 20 minutes
Needed: A PC with Internet access
Reference: Pages 640-641 of the textbook

1. PING your computer by IP address. Record the results in the space below:

2. PING your computer using the loopback address.

3. PING the IP address of an Internet host. Record the results in the space below:

4. PING the fully qualified domain name of an Internet host. Compare the results with those received in Step 4. Record the results in the space below:

5. PING a host until manually stopped.

6. Record the route for count hops.

Project 19C: Use Address Resolution Protocol

Time to Complete: 30 minutes
Needed: A PC connected to a network.
Reference: Pages 642-645 of the textbook

1. Display the ARP cache. Record the results in the space below:

2. PING several computers on the network.

3. Display the ARP cache again. Record the results in the space below:

4. Add a host to ARP cache.

Project 19D: Use Netstat

Time to Complete: 30 minutes

Needed: A PC connected to a network

Reference: Pages 645-647 of the textbook

1. Show the routing table that is displayed on your local machine. Record the results in the space below:

2. Display all connections and listening ports. Record the results in the space below:

3. Display Ethernet statistics. Record the results in the space below:

4. Display addresses and port numbers in numerical form. Record the results in the space below:

5. Display the owning process ID associated with each connection. Record the results in the space below:

Project 19E: Use Nbtstat

Time to Complete: 30 minutes

Needed: A PC connected to a network.

Reference: Pages 647-648 of the textbook

1. List a remote machine's name table. Record the results in the space below:

2. List the contents of NBT's cache by machine names and IP address. Record the results in the space below:

3. List local NetBIOS names. Record the results in the space below:

4. If a WINS server is available on your network, display a list of names resolved by broadcast and WINS.

Project 19F: Use IPCONFIG

Time to Complete: 30 minutes
Needed: A PC with Internet access, running a compatible Windows operating system.
Reference: Pages 648-651 of the textbook

1. Display all IP configuration information for your computer. Print the results and attach them to this page.

2. Release your DHCP assigned IP addressing information.

3. Renew your DHCP assigned addressing information. Record the results of this renewal in the space provided below:

Project 19G: Use WINIPCFG

Time to Complete: 30 minutes

Needed: A PC with Internet access, running a compatible Windows operating system.

Reference: Pages 652-653 of the textbook

1. Display all IP configuration information for your computer. Print the results and attach them to this form.

2. Release your DHCP assigned IP addressing information.

3. Renew your DHCP assigned addressing information. Record the results of this renewal in the space provided below:

20 Troubleshooting Small Office/ Home Office Network Failures

Small office/home office, or *SOHO*, as it is more commonly known, is a term that has been coined in the past few years and was spawned largely by network users who were telecommuting or working out of their homes. In the SOHO environment, many users connect to some type of network remotely. That is, they are not connected directly to the network. Instead, they connect indirectly, or on demand. Students at all levels should work through these exercises to ensure they understand how to properly troubleshoot these types of failures.

Project 20A: Shop for DSL Service

Time to Complete: 20 minutes
Needed: A PC with Internet access, telephone
Reference: Pages 669-672 of the textbook

Shop your local area to obtain information about DSL service for home office users. Record your findings in the space provided below:

- Available: Yes or No?

- Service plans available: (Record uplink speeds, downlink speeds, and cost.)

- Is it available at your residence?

- Hardware provided? (Identify which is provided or must be purchased. If you must purchase the hardware, obtain information about the cost for each component.)

- Will the provider allow you to do the installation: Yes or No?

- Installation fee?

- Services provided: (Personal web pages, number of e-mail identities, etc.)

- Length of contract required?

Project 20B: Connect a Personal Computer to DSL Service

Time to Complete: 30 minutes
Needed: A PC, network interface card, DSL line, DSL modem or router, cables
Reference: Pages 672-675 of the textbook

1. After obtaining the necessary service from your provider, establish the physical connection.
2. Install a network interface card in the computer. After the card is installed, start the computer and install the appropriate driver when prompted.
3. Install and configure a client and the necessary protocols.
4. Connect the network card into a DSL modem or router.
5. Connect the modem or router into a telephone wall jack.
6. Test the connection.

Project 20C: Shop for Cable Service

Time to Complete: 20 minutes
Needed: A PC with Internet access, telephone
Reference: Pages 675-677 of the textbook

Shop your local area to obtain information about **cable modem and DSL service** for home office users. Record your findings in the space provided below:

- Available: Yes or No?

- Service plans available: (Record uplink speeds, downlink speeds, and cost.)

- Hardware provided? (Identify which is provided or must be purchased. If you must purchase the hardware, obtain information about the cost for each component.)

- Will the provider allow you to do the installation: Yes or No?

- Installation fee?

- Services provided: (Personal web pages, number of e-mail identities, etc.)

- Length of contract required?

Project 20D: Connect a Personal Computer to a Cable Service

Time to Complete: 30 minutes
Needed: A PC, network interface card, cable line, cable modem or router, splitter, cables
Reference: Pages 666-677 of the textbook

1. Cut the cable and attach a splitter, only if necessary.
2. Run one piece of cable to a television if necessary. Run another cable to the cable modem.
3. Connect the cable modem to a network interface card in a computer.

Project 20E: Shop for Satellite Service

Time to Complete: 20 minutes
Needed: A PC with Internet access, telephone
Reference: Pages 679-680 of the textbook

Shop your local area to obtain information about **satellite service** for home office users. Record your findings in the space provided below:

• Available: Yes or No?

• Service plans available: (Record uplink speeds, downlink speeds, and cost.)

• Is it available at your residence?

- Hardware provided? (Identify which is provided or must be purchased. If you must purchase the hardware, obtain information about the cost for each component.)

- Will the provider allow you to do the installation: Yes or No?

- Installation fee?

- Services provided: (Personal web pages, number of e-mail identities, etc.)

- Length of contract required?

Project 20F: Connect a Personal Computer to a Wireless Network

Time to Complete: 30 minutes

Needed: A PC or laptop, wireless network interface card, wireless access point which is connected to a network

Reference: Pages 682-683 of the textbook

1. Install the wireless network card into the computer. Install the appropriate drivers if prompted.
2. Install the software necessary to access the network
3. If necessary, connect the wireless access point to the wired network.
4. Test the wireless network.
5. If there is a problem connecting with an AP, check the signal strength or relocate the client computer.

Project 20G: Create an Ad Hoc Wireless Network

Time to Complete: 20 minutes
Needed: Two compatible PDAs
Reference: Pages 682-683 of the textbook

1. Move the PDAs close, with their infrared ports facing each other.
2. Using instructions provided by the manufacturer, prepare the devices to transfer a file.
3. Transfer the file.
4. Confirm that the transfer occurred.

Project 20H: Troubleshoot a Modem with AT Commands

Time to Complete: 30 minutes
Needed: A computer with an installed modem, connected to a phone line
Reference: Pages 686-689 of the textbook

1. Use AT commands to check functions on your modem. (Be aware that some commands may not work with all modems.)
2. Reset the modem to default factory settings.
3. Set the modem speaker to the lowest volume.
4. Set the modem speaker to the highest volume.
5. Tell Windows to report your true connection speed.
6. Tell the modem to check for a dial tone before it starts dialing.